beginnings &
beyond

The poems in this collection were previously published in the following books:

Beginnings
The Search
The Growing Season
Widening View
Women I Have Known and Been
Picture Window

beginnings & beyond

AN ANTHOLOGY OF POETRY

CAROL LYNN PEARSON

Cedar Fort, Inc.
Springville, Utah

ISBN: 1-55517-870-7
v.1

Published by Cedar Fort,
an imprint of Cedar Fort, Inc.
925 N. Main Springville, Utah, 84663
www.cedarfort.com

Distributed by:

Cover design by Nicole Williams
Cover design © 2005 by Lyle Mortimer

Printed in the United States of America
10 9 8 7 6 5 4 3 2 1

Printed on acid-free paper

contents

1 OUR DIVINE JOURNEY

2 GOD AND ETERNITY

6 FRIENDS AND RELATIONSHIPS

7 WOMEN

8 MEN AND WOMEN

9 MOTHERHOOD, PREGNANCY AND BIRTH

10 ADOPTION

11 PARENTHOOD AND CHILD RAISING

12 ADVERSITY

our divine journey

BEGINNINGS

Today
You came running
With a small specked egg
Warm in your hand.
You could barely understand
I know
As I told you
Of Beginnings—
Of egg and bird;
Told, too,
That years ago
You began
Smaller than sight.
And then
As egg yearns for sky
And seed
Stretches to tree
You became
Like me.

Oh
But there's
So much more.
You and I
Child
Have just begun.

Think:
Worlds from now
What might we be—
We
Who are seed
Of Deity.

OPTICAL ILLUSION

Time is a stage magician
Pulling sleight-of-hand tricks
To make you think things go.

There
Eclipsed by the quick scarf
A lifetime of loves.

Zip—
The child is man.
Zip—
The friend in your arms
Is earth.
Zip—
The green tree is gold, is white,
Is smoking ash, is gone.

Zip—
Time's trick goes on.
All things loved—
Now you see them, now you don't.

Oh, this world has more
Of coming and of going
Than I can bear.
I guess it's eternity I want,
Where all things are
And always will be,
Where I can hold my loves
A little looser,
Where finally we realize
Time
Is the only thing that really dies.

CREATION CONTINUED

I will continue
To create the universe today
Right where God left off.

Little pockets of chaos
Somehow survived the ordering
And I feel moved
To move upon them
As in the beginning
The Spirit of God moved
Upon the face of the waters.

I will move upon my backyard today
And the weeds will be subdued
And the flowers can grow
And it will be good.

I will move long-distance
Upon a broken heart
And leave a little balm
And it will be good.

I will move upon
The hunger of my children
With salad and spaghetti
Which is Emily's favorite
And it will be good
And even they will say so.
And I will move too
Upon their minds
Leaving a little poem
Or an important thought
And that will be even better
Though they won't say so.

I will move upon
Birth defects and cancer
With five and ten dollar checks
To help the scientists
Who are battling the big chaos
And I will move upon world hunger
With a twenty-four dollar check
For little Marilza in Brazil
And it will be good.

I will move upon
The kitchen floor
And the dirty laundry
And a blank piece of paper
And at the end of the day
Have a little creation to show.

And the evening and the morning
Are my eighteen thousand
And ninety-sixth day
And tomorrow will start another one.
And here is chaos and there is chaos
And who knows if creation
Will finally be done?

THE CAST

I lost the starring part in "Our Town"
To Linda, a girl not half as good as me,
Who kept her eyes down
For the whole tryout, and even stuttered.

When the cast was posted
And the high school drama coach
Saw me reading it through my tears,
He put an arm around me and said,
"Now, look—things are not always as they
     appear.
This is not Broadway;
It's an educational institution.
We're here for two reasons—to put on a show,
And, more important, to help people grow.
Someday you'll see."

So Linda played Emily,
And she didn't even stutter.
And I was Third Woman at the Wedding,
Watching and wondering how he knew
What she could really do
If she had the chance.

Since then I have guessed that God,
Being a whole lot smarter
Than my high school drama coach,
Might be offstage sometimes
With an arm around a questioning cast:
"Now, don't try to outguess me.
Sometimes the first shall be last
And the last shall be first.
Mortality is an educational institution.
We've got to put on the show,

And, too, we've got to help people grow."

As I walk through the scenes
Watch the costumes move and listen to the
    lines
Of the powerful, the weak, the rich, the poor,
I look at the leads with less awe than most,
And at the spear-carriers with more.

URGENT TO MARILYN

Marilyn had a job—
Working out her salvation.
It wasn't nine to five,
It was nine to nine
In twenty-four-hour shifts.

And there was no vacation,
And in case she should get fired
Nobody else was hiring,
So Marilyn worked hard
And she worked fast
And she worked in fear.

The boss was away a lot
And Marilyn wondered
If he liked her work,
And not knowing, she worked harder.
She did everything on every list
Twice over to make sure.

She didn't have much fun
On the job.
It was more the retirement
Benefits she was there for,
The mansion, the glory.

On a typical day
She ran frantically from
The school committee chairperson department
To the carpool department
To the physical fitness
Department.

She even stopped running
Past the yoga and meditation department
And sat long enough
To cross that off her list.

And then she ran
To the home beautification department
Ran with scriptures on cassette in one hand
And self-help in the other.

Ran because there were
Twenty-two minutes left to fill,
Ran past the boss's memo
On the bulletin board:

"Urgent to Marilyn:
Peace, be still."

OF THE MYSTERIES

I know only as much of God and the world
As a creature with two eyes must;
But what I do understand, I love
And what I don't understand, I trust.

THE LESSON

Yes, my fretting
Frowning child,
I could cross
The room to you
More easily.
But I've already
Learned to walk
So I make you
Come to me.

Let go, now—
There!
You see?

Oh, remember
This simple lesson,
Child,
And when
In later years
You cry out
With tight fists
And tears
"Oh, help me,
God, please—"
Just listen
And you'll hear
A silent voice:

"I would, child,
I would.
But I know
It's you, not I,
Who needs to grow."

PROVISION FOR THE END

What to do when
The dawn brings night
And the moon spins out
And the stars fall white?

Wait calm in the silence
The black sky spilled:
Your lamp will light—
If it is filled.

PERSPECTIVE FROM MORTALITY

My life is patterned as the palm
Of a rain-washed leaf, calm
Cut and full.
But
I view my life from underneath
Which—like the patterned leaf—
Is fuzzed and dull.

WITHIN

I read a map once
Saying the kingdom of God
Was within me
But I never trusted
Such unlikely ground.

I went out.
I scoured schools
And libraries
And chapels and temples
And other people's eyes
And the skies and the rocks,
And I found treasures
From the kingdom's treasury
But not the kingdom.

Finally I came in quiet
For a rest
And turned on the light.

And there
Just like a surprise party
Was all the smiling royalty,
King, Queen, court.

People have been
Locked up for less, I know.
But I tell you
Something marvelous
Is bordered by this skin:

I am a castle
And the kingdom of God
Is within.

THE FAMILY OF LIGHT

Kindled into the family
That sparked the sun
We came—
With suns and moons and stars
In us forever.

And the Mother
Who nurtures new light
In the warmest of all wombs,
And the Father
Who holds in His hands
The growing glow and blows it brighter—
Together placed us in another room.

It is dark here.
Deep within element
We dim and dim.
And to slim the ray
That might find its way out
We handcraft clever bushels
Of modest, fashionable fears.

But long darkness is untenable
And we yearn for the burning
To begin again.

We have had too much night.
Shall we—
Shall we together shed our bushels
And stand revealed—
Sons and daughters of light?

god and eternity

UNPINNED

I hope that humans
Never pin down
Love or God.

Things pinned down
(Like butterflies)
Lose something
(Like life).

I can go with progress.
I am grateful
For a long life span
For medicine and computers
And I'm glad to know
The layout of the
Galaxy.

But let some
Mysteries win.

Let love and God be free
As a million monarchs
To touch our faces
With bright wings
And leave wonder in our eyes
As they rise
From the hand-held pin.

THE REASON

A certain panic
Finds me
When I see
A forest, a train
A library.
So many trees to touch
Places
Faces yet to view
And, too
So many words to read.

If I concede
All space to earth
All time to life
The disproportion
Is absurd
(My tiny taste
And the giant waste
Of all creation
I've not known).
What a wretched
Faithless view
Of God's economy.

It isn't true.
The forest, the train
The library—
Are why we have
Eternity.

THE BENEFICIARY

I was not there.
But they say
It happened for me.
On the cross it happened
And in the tomb.
For me—
Vicariously.

But how?
It was His sacrifice
Not mine.
It was He who wept
Who bled
Not me.

Except—
Why, look—
At the flick of a finger
I instantly receive
What Edison
Gave his full life
To achieve.

Perhaps
If one man
Searching the skies
Willed us the key
To conquer night—
May not another
A greater
Bequeath from the cross
The key to
Eternal light?

MILK BEFORE MEAT

Why worry on
Exactly how
A body will arise
Once someone dies?

I can't even
Understand
The manifest things—
Like how
A seagull flies
From merely
Having wings.

TO AN ATHEIST

God must have a huge sense of humor
So righteously to resist
The temptation of turning the tables
On your pretending He does not exist.

TO A BELOVED SKEPTIC

I cannot talk with you of God
Since sober wise you grew;
So my one recourse in charity
Is to talk with God of you.

THE SOURCE

If God is love
The source
The spring
Should not the lover
Pilgrimage there—
Reverently
Seeking supply?—

That the cup he gives
Will not be dry.

THE WATCHERS

There is a tomb
In old Jerusalem
Where one is told
Christ spent
Death's interim,
And many walk
That way
In curiosity.

"Three days
Behind the stone,"
He said,
"And then
A longer time
In heaven before
I come again."

But few
There are
Who watch
That door.

THE OFFERING

For ancient wrongs
God required
The burning of flesh
An offering fresh
From the flocks.

But Christ turned
The outside in.
And for my sin
God demands
The harder part:
No yearling lamb
On the altar
But my own
Wounded heart.

prayer

AFFIRMATION

Some
Heaven-sought answers
Come in sound—
A voice perhaps—
But I have found
Mine always come
In utter silence.

My heart
A swollen sea
Stops tearing
At its shores
And gradually stills.

The whipping
Of the wind
The gull's sharp cry—
All sounds
Cease.

I listen
To the answer.

Silence
Speaks clearly:
It speaks peace.

THOUGHTS IN THE CHAPEL

How I will
Greet the Lord
In heaven
I do not know.

But here
With the Sabbath organ
And Sabbath bread,
Or at home
Beside my bed—
Whenever we converse
Just Him and me
(Watching the sunset
Or the sea)
I can at least
Rehearse.

PRAYER

This radio set
Called prayer
Is designed
For remarkably
Simple repair.
When the lines fail
There is no doubt
Which half
Of the set
Is out.

THE USES OF PRAYER

Heaven
Holds out the blessing
Like a bright
Ripe fruit
Only waiting
For us to ask it:

Our words
Weave the basket.

GUILT

I have no vulture sins, God
That overhang my sky
To climb, grey-feathering the air
And swoop carnivorously.

It's just the tiny sins, God
That from memory appear
Like tedious, buzzing flies to dart
Like static through my prayer.

PRAYER AT TABLE

The food, yes—
But most of all
Bless
Me.
The bread is
Full and good
As I would be.
Oh, Lord,
My only leaven,
Work
Warm me
Let me lift
Toward heaven.

growth and
self-development

THE GROWING SEASON

A wound in my roots
From a zealous hoe

The quick demise
Of friendly weeds

A strange new stretching
With the flow
Of nourishment
From last year's leaves.

Sun and rain
By turns appear:

Growing season
Must be here.

INDEPENDENCE

I would stay here
Close to roots
That fed me
Close to
Cool shelter—

Always close
I would be.

Except,
I'm afraid.

Have you seen
The pitiful
Small green
That grows
In shade?

ON GOING BACK

Cry or threaten
Or bribe or beg

A chicken cannot
Peck its way back
Into the egg.

MY SEASON

Seeing the tree
Beneath a baptism of snow
You may call her barren.
But is it so?
And for all your watchings
On a March night
When the twigs seem dark
And the bark
Feels cold to your hand—
Can you call her fruitless
And so leave?

She smiles.
Calm in the station
Of seasons
And in the ordination
Of sun and sap and spring.

As for me?
You turn away
Impatient with
The promises you've seen.
But—inside I fill
And pulse and flow
With the urgency of green.

I've a season
Like the tree.
And all your
Faithless doubts
Will not destroy
The rising spring
In me.

POWER

When she learned that she
Didn't have to plug into
Someone or something
Like a toaster into a wall

When she learned that she
Was a windmill and had only
To raise her arms
To catch the universal whisper
And turn

        turn

            turn

She moved.

Oh, she moved
And her dance was a marvel.

JOURNAL

Put the thought
In words
And the words in ink
In a page in a book
In a very private place
Like under a mattress.

A sacred process
Wonderful as alchemy
Is at work
Even in the dark
While you sleep
Making something better
Than history:

Understanding.

THE LITTLE TREES

When she was small
She used to call
Them the little trees—
Those sapling cottonwoods
A dozen or so
On the hill above the spring.

After a day's play with cousins
She would hear her mother
Calling from the door,
"Supper's almost done—
Come a runnin'."

And she would make
Her usual request:
"Please, Ma, can I walk them
To the little trees?
I'll run right back."

"All right. Hurry along."

So she would walk her cousins
To the little trees
And wave them on.

And then—
She was the one at the door
That same door, calling,
"Time to come in now
All of you
Quick as a wink.
Tell your cousins good-bye."

"Please, Mother, can we walk them
Just to the big trees?
We'll go so fast."

She watched them
Walk their cousins
To the big trees—
Those blazing green cottonwoods
A dozen or so
On the hill above the spring.

Rooted at the door
She watched them go.
And from somewhere
A wind blew through her—
The awesome thrill
Of things that grow.

NEW HANDS

Celia got drinking from her mother
And hitting from her father
And yelling from both
Like she got pizza crusts for breakfast.

And she took it all in
And digested it and became it
Because you are what you eat.

And her parents
Ate from the table of their parents
Who ate from the table of theirs
Back and back and back
And Celia was stuck.

But cells die
And every seven years we are new.

Celia's new heart and new hands
Set the table and stir the pot
And serve better stuff than she ever got.

TURNING

I turn
But not away.

Toward
(Like a sunflower)
Light
Warmth.
I turn toward life.

The decision
Is in my roots
And is deep.

You are free
To face the ground
If you have no will
To lift
And I will be sad.

I am willing to be sad
But not to be dead
And so I turn.

A WIDENING VIEW

When my eye first opened
Behind the viewfinder,
There in closeup
Was a flower—
The only possible flower.

Who turned the lens
For the pullback?
Life, I guess.
What—
Another flower?
And another?
A field alive with flowers.
(The only possible field?)

Loss.
Delight.

Borders are forever gone.
Life is at the lens.
The view goes on
And on.

life's little lessons

FROM THE PHILOSOPHER

Can it be
In this huge
Hunger to know

I try so hard to see backstage
I miss the best parts
Of the show?

GETTING READY

He's always getting ready
But never quite goes.
He's always taking notes
But never quite knows.

He's touched by all the starving
But doesn't touch his wife.
His life is spent at meetings
But he never meets life.

CONNECTION

Incredible
That I have spent
All these seasons
Staring upward to see

How the tree
Fits the leaf
Instead of how
The leaf fits the tree.

WORDS

I wanted to know
What it felt like to swear.

So one day
Away out in the back pasture where
Two horses switched
For the big flies,
I stood on a little bridge
Took a deep breath
And said every bad word
I'd ever heard.

The horse tails switched on
And on ran the unpolluted stream.

It took about a week though
To wash and rinse
My mouth clean
And I've never said those words since—

Though now I'm counting
Many another word
I should have taken
To where only horses heard.

AT THE CHURCH CHRISTMAS PARTY

My little Johnny, who was three,
Climbed with lights in his eyes onto Santa's
  knee.
"And what would you like this year, my boy?
If I can I'll bring your favorite toy."

Johnny didn't even need time to think.
"I want a dolly," he said, "that will eat and
  drink."
Twelve parents, at least, turned to look at me
And a big man said suspiciously,

"Next year he'll want a dress or two."
I replied, "It's the father in him coming
  through."
"Well, that's not what some folks would say.
A kid's character's built by the way he'll play."

My little Johnny, who was three,
Climbed with lights in his eyes from Santa's
  knee.
And the big man grinned as he watched his
  son
Ask Santa Claus for a tank and a gun.

THE UNWRITTEN POEM

Sometimes
In a sitting down moment
On a day
Of stove-heating and sad-irons
And layering newspaper between
Quilts to keep us warmer
I heard my mother say,
"I wish I had time to write a poem."
And then she would start
The potatoes.

When I was twelve
A thing happened that
Broke my heart—
A school thing I've forgotten now.
For hours I cried my humiliation
Into a handkerchief.

Next day my mother
Brought it in from ironing
That handkerchief
And gave it to me special.
"Here," she laid it in my lap.
"You've had it in happy times and in sad.
There'll be more of both.
Keep it, and it will remind you
The better follows the bad."

She went back to ironing
And my fingers traced
The little flowers of fading blue.

I can remember other poems
She left me, too.

THE GRADE

God does not grade
On the curve,
I'm sure of it.

But we sit around
Like high school students
In an important class
Whose teacher has drawn
On the blackboard
The tiny wedges for the A's and the F's
And the great bulge for the C's.

We sigh in veiled relief
As the person down the row messes up
Because it makes us look better
And probably means an F
For him, which is good
Because while we have
Nothing against him personally
It means an A is more
Available to us.

And we secretly sorrow
When the person in front of us
Does really well
Although we like her okay
Because there goes another good grade
Darn it, and we're looking worse and worse
And slipping further down the curve.

And God, I think
Sits at the front of the class
Holding A's enough for all
Watching us work out our salvation
In fear and competition.

TOO BUSY

It was time
To prune the apricots.
"Only one bud
Every few inches of tree
Or they won't grow,"
Said my father.

I didn't believe him
Though
And I kept one branch
All full of flowers
For I knew
They would all
Be beautiful and bright
And big—
Ever so big.

Early one morning
In fruit time
I ran to the orchard
And beneath
The heavy-hanging
Golden crop
I harvested my apricots,
My many, many
Tiny apricots.

When it was dark
I fed them
To the cow.

I prune now.

friends and
relationships

SUPPORT GROUP

You can fall here.
We are a quilt set to catch you
A quilt of women's hands
Threaded by pain made useful.

With generations of comfort-making
Behind us, we offer this gift
Warm as grandma's feather bed
Sweet as the Heavenly Mother's
Lullaby song.

You can fall here.
Women's hands are strong.

ALL US MILLIONS

Divided by darkness
Blended by the sun—
Through some amazing mathematics
We come out
One.

THE FRIEND

Let me
Be the hearth
Where you sit
To work your clay.
I'll not say
"Shape it like this
Or like that,"
I promise.

Let me watch
As you
In absolute agency
Mold your
Mortal dream.

Only
Sit close
And let me give
A little light
A little warmth.
Yes
Warmth especially.

Cold clay yields
To no form.
Let me
Be your hearth.
Sit close
Be warm.

THE FORGIVING

Forgive?
Will I forgive,
You cry.
But
What is the gift
The favor?

You would lift
Me from
My poor place
To stand beside
The Savior.
You would have
Me see with
His eyes
Smile
And with Him
Reach out to
Salve
A sorrowing heart—
For one small
Moment
To share in
Christ's great art.

Will I forgive,
You cry.
Oh
May I—
May I?

JOHNNY'S SHOES

He read the Johnny-sized words
And I read the big ones:

"Love your enemies
Do good to them that hate you
And pray for them
Which despitefully use you."

He knelt for evening prayer
Pure as Johnny is always pure:

"Heavenly Father,
Thank you for the good day
That we've had
And please bless the person
Who stole my shoes at the
Swimming pool today that he
Won't have to steal anymore
And that he can have more
Love inside of him . . ."

Out the window
Or through the wall
(I wasn't quick enough to see)
Shot some small share
Of enormous wealth
Never to be stolen
Never to lose.

And somebody somewhere
Instantly wore more than
Johnny's shoes.

HER FATHER'S TEARS

She was always embarrassed
When her father cried
For it was so unmanly
And she always knew
When it would happen.

When he read the note
From Mrs. Lewis
Saying what a joy she was
To have in class
And how proud of her
He must be

When they brought in
A fifty-candled cake
And sang him a surprise

When the six o'clock news
Showed the kidnapped returned
Or the hostage released
Or the flag at half mast

He would reach for his handkerchief
Folded and white
And dab his left eye
Then his right
And she would *just die!*

She grew up, of course, and would now
If she could reach across the years
Fill a flask
With the holy water
Of her father's tears.

UNFED

We feed one another
In rations,
Serve affection
Measured to
The minimum daily
Requirement,
The very acceptable
Least—

While love
Bursts the walls
Of our larder
Wondering
Amazed
Why we are afraid
To feast.

THE WASTE

They're dumping wheat
Into the sea,
And oranges too
I hear.

Just like my heart
That annually
Wastes fields of love
For fear.

THE SUNFLOWER

Of course you have clouds.
What mortal sky does not?
Only in heaven
Are the heavens clear forever.

It's all right.
I am a sunflower.
I will find the light.

PREJUDICE

The celestial soul
Bigger than boundaries
Extends
Past labels of name
Or place or shade.

It will take
I think
A long time
To learn how.

Should we not
Start now?

SPLIT

You felt safe
I know
In that little space
Laced with love.
Your cocoon
You called it
Warm
Warm.
I cried with you
When it split.

Oh, safe
Cannot compare with sky.
I like you so much better
As a butterfly.

THE LIGHTHOUSE

Do you know
How many count on you
To steer by this night?

Do you know
How dark the sea
And dim the stars
And strong the wind
Out there?

And you would
Hide your lighthouse
Under a bushel?

Don't you dare!

THE DAYS WE SHARED

They were generating days
The days we shared
Bright as when
Two fires combine.

I leave
Wearing some of your light
As you leave
Wearing some of mine.

TO THE ONE WHO HAS BEEN DONE DIRT

Cry or curse or call it unfair
But be grateful till the grave
That in this hurt
You're the one who received
And not the one who gave.

THE NOURISHER

Without recipe
Without dish
You bring a banquet.

You step into a room
Open, mix, bake and serve.
Instantly the feast is spread.

Instantly
I am fed.

LET GO

When you're giving birth
Let go.

When you're watching at death
Let go.

Whenever a life needs
A life apart
Hold your heart.
Let go.

women

ON NEST BUILDING

Mud is not bad for nest building.
Mud and sticks
And a fallen feather or two will do
And require no reaching.
I could rest there with my tiny ones
Sound for the season, at least.

But
If I may fly awhile—
If I may cut through a sunset going out
And a rainbow coming back
Color upon color sealed in my eyes—
If I may have the unboundaried skies
For my study
Clouds, cities, rivers for my rooms—
If I may search the centuries
For melody and meaning—
If I may try for the sun—

I shall come back
Bearing such beauties
Gleaned from God's and the world's very best.
I shall come filled.

And then—
Oh, the nest that I can build!

BAKING BREAD

There seemed more accusation
Than admiration in Vivian's voice
When she said,
"Well, I wish *I* had time
To bake bread!"

And so sometimes when
The loaves were in the oven
And Vivian was at the door
Louise mumbled something about
Another bake sale again

And never even tried to explain
Her near-religious ritual:

How the flour on her fingers
Was the sun and the rain
And the earth

How the thump of her palms
On the dough
Was the dance of women
On the ancient threshing floor

How the smell of the baking
Leavened her
And left her believing that
We rise, we rise

And how the cutting
Of the first warm slice
For the first child home
Made her a bounteous goddess
With life in her hand.

MILLIE'S MOTHER'S RED DRESS

It hung there in the closet
While she was dying, Mother's red dress
Like a gash in the row
Of dark, old clothes
She had worn away her life in.

They had called me home
And I knew when I saw her
She wasn't going to last.

When I saw the dress, I said,
"Why, Mother—how beautiful!
I've never seen it on you."

"I've never worn it," she slowly said.
"Sit down, Millie—I'd like to undo
A lesson or two before I go, if I can."

I sat by her bed
And she sighed a bigger breath
Than I thought she could hold.
"Now that I'll soon be gone
I can see some things.
Oh, I taught you good—but I taught you
  wrong."

"What do you mean, Mother?"

"Well—I always thought
That a good woman never takes her turn
That she's just for doing for somebody else.
Do here, do there, always keep
Everybody else's wants tended and make sure
Yours are at the bottom of the heap.

Maybe someday you'll get to them
But of course you never do.
My life was like that—doing for your dad
Doing for the boys, for your sisters, for you."

"You did—everything a mother could."

"Oh, Millie, Millie, it was no good—
For you—for him. Don't you see?
I did you the worst of wrongs.
I asked nothing—for me!

"Your father in the other room
All stirred up and staring at the walls—
When the doctor told him, he took
It bad—came to my bed and all but shook
The life right out of me. 'You can't die,
Do you hear? What'll become of me?
What'll become of me?'
It'll be hard, all right, when I go.
He can't even find the frying pan, you know.

"And you children.
I was a free ride for everybody, everywhere.
I was the first one up and the last one down
Seven days out of the week.
I always took the toast that got burned,
And the very smallest piece of pie.
I look at how some of your brothers treat their
   wives now,
And it makes me sick, 'cause it was me
That taught it to them. And they learned.
They learned that a woman doesn't
Even exist except to give.
Why, every single penny that I could save
Went for your clothes or your books

Even when it wasn't necessary.
Can't even remember once when I took
Myself downtown to buy something
    beautiful—
For me.

"Except last year when I got that red dress.
I found I had twenty dollars
That wasn't especially spoke for.
I was on my way to pay it extra on the washer.
But somehow—I came home with this big
    box.
Your father really gave it to me then.
'Where you going to wear a thing like that
        to—
Some opera or something?'
And he was right, I guess.
I've never, except in the store,
Put on that dress.

"Oh, Millie—I always thought if you take
Nothing for yourself in this world
You'd have it all in the next somehow.
I don't believe that anymore.
I think the Lord wants us to have
    something—
Here—and now.

"And I'm telling you, Millie, if some miracle
Could get me off this bed, you could look
For a different mother, 'cause I would be one.
Oh, I passed up my turn so long
I would hardly know how to take it.
But I'd learn, Millie.
I would learn!"

It hung there in the closet
While she was dying, Mother's red dress
Like a gash in the row
Of dark, old clothes
She had worn away her life in.

Her last words to me were these:
"Do me the honor, Millie,
Of not following in my footsteps.
Promise me that."

I promised.
She caught her breath
Then Mother took her turn
In death.

THE STEWARD

Heber looked at his lands
And he was pleased.
He'd be leaving them tomorrow, and his
   hands
Hurt with anticipated idleness.
But he knew there was no other way
When a man is seventy-eight and has to make
Two rest stops with a full bucket of milk
Between the barn and the kitchen.
Condominiums—do they have gardens?
He wondered.
His son had arranged the place for them in
   town
And he was ready. He sat down
On the rock that knew his body
Better than the front room chair.

Could it really be fifty-five years ago
That sitting there
They had talked?
His father's voice had never left him:
"Heber, I'm trusting to you
The most precious thing I've got.
I worked hard for this land. You know all
   about
The crickets and the Indians and the drought
And the buckets of sweat it took
To make what you see today.
I'm giving it to you as a stewardship, son.
And when your time with the land is done
And we get together again
I'm going to call you to account.
I'm going to say, 'Heber, did you make it more

Than you found it? Did you watch it
And tend it? Did you make it grow?
Is it everything it can be?'
That's what I'll want to know."

Heber looked out on the fields
That for fifty-five years had been
Green and gold in proper turn—
On the fences and the barns and the ditches
And the trees in careful rows.
Even his father hadn't been able to get
     peaches.
He could hardly wait to report about those.

Margaret was finishing the last closet.
Just a few things were going to the city
And the rest rose in a mountain
On the back porch, waiting for the children
To sort through and take what they chose.
She opened the lid on a shoebox of valentines.
Perhaps just one or two for memory's sake?
But whose—whose would she take?

She put the box aside and reached again.
"What in the world?" In an instant her face
Cleared and in her hands was the old familiar
     case.
The violin. She hadn't touched it for forty
     years
Hadn't thought of it for twenty at least.
Well, there they finally were—the tears.
Her mother's dishes hadn't done it
Or the little Bible she had almost buried with
     Ellen
Or the valentines—
But there they were for the violin.

She picked up the bow.
Had it always been so thin?
Perhaps her hand had grown so used to big
    things
To kettles that weighed ten pounds empty
And to milk cans and buckets of coal.

The wood felt smooth against her chin
As she put the bow to a string.
A slow, startled sound wavered then fell.
How did she used to tune it? Ah, well,
No sense wasting time on moving day.
If Heber should come in he would say,
"Well, there's Margaret—fiddlin' around
With her fiddle again."
He'd always said it with a smile, though.

"I could have done it," she said out loud.
"And it wouldn't have hurt him.
It wouldn't have hurt anybody!"

He hadn't minded that she'd practiced two
    hours
Every afternoon—after all, she got up at five
And nobody in the world could criticize
The way she kept the house
Or the care she gave to the children.
And he was proud that she was asked
To play twice a year at the church.
And music made her so happy.
If she missed a day things were not quite
So bright around the house.
Even Heber noticed that.

And then she was invited to join
The symphony in town.

Oh, to play with a real orchestra again!
In a hall with a real audience again!

"But, Margaret, isn't that too much to ask
Of a woman with children and a farm to
     tend?"

"Oh, Heber, I'll get up at four if I have to.
I won't let down—not a bit. I promise!"

"But I couldn't drive you in,
Not two nights a week all year round,
And more when they're performing."

"I can drive, Heber. It's only twenty miles.
I'd be fine. You would have to be
With the children, though, until Ellen
Is a little older."

"But I couldn't guarantee two nights a week—
Not with my responsibilities to the farm
And to the church."

"Heber, there's no way to tell you
How important this is to me. Please, Heber
I'll get up at four if I have to."

But Heber said no.
What if something happened to the car?
And then it just wouldn't look right
For a man's wife to be out chasing
Around like that. What would it lead to next?
Once in a while he read of some woman
Who went so far with her fancy notions
That she up and left her family, children and
     all.

He couldn't see Margaret ever doing that
But it's best to play it safe.
Two nights a week—that was asking a lot.

So Heber said no.
It was his responsibility to take care of her.

She had been given to him, in fact.
He remembered the ceremony well
The pledges, the rings
And he didn't take it lightly.
She had been given to him
And it was up to him to decide these things.
So Heber said no.
She had seemed to take it all right
Though she was quieter than usual
And more and more an afternoon would pass
Without her practicing.

He didn't really notice how it happened—
The shrinking of her borders
The drying up of her green.
If Heber ever thought about it in later years
He marked it up to the twins.
Motherhood was hard on a woman
And Margaret just wasn't quite the same as
    before.

She laid the violin in its case
And rubbed away the small wet drop
On her thin hand.

"I could have done it," she said aloud.
"Heber, you didn't understand.
I could have done it and not hurt anybody.
I would have gotten up at four!"

Slowly she made her way to the porch
And put the violin with the things
For the children to sort through.

"Will any of them remember?
I don't think so."

Heber gave a last look at his lands
And he was pleased.
He could face his father with a clear mind.
"Here's my stewardship," he would say,
"And I think you'll find
I did everything you asked.
I took what you gave me—and I made it
    more."

He got up and started toward the house.
Putting to his lips
A long, thin piece of hay.
"Better get movin'. Margaret will be
Needing me for supper right away."

THROW IT AWAY

The bottles were lined up
Like little soldiers on the bathroom sink.
Sara had ranked them by strength.
The red ones were the killers
And would be sent first
Backed by the green
And then the white.
Together they were the good army
She needed to get it done right.

Left was the half bottle
That had been in the cabinet for years
Which she had got for the biopsy that time
And now a soldier too weak to fight.

She pried off the lid and watched the pills
Drop into the toilet in a single splash.

Empty, powerless, useless.
Throw them away!

She tossed the bottle into the trash.
And her turn was next.

Powerless! She had always been powerless.
Or had she once been potent
But had sat on the shelf too long?

She remembered—was it her?—a girl
Who could run a mile after two dance classes
And stand up to the fourth grade bully
And heal a hamster's broken leg
With a splint and a song.

She remembered a woman who could
Write an "A" paper at two A.M.
And climb a mountain on the steepest side
With more than her share of food on her back
And leave twenty-five love-notes
All over the apartment for a roommate
Whose mother had died.

If that was her it was another lifetime.
She had traded herself for him
And done it gladly for she loved him so.
She overflowed with him
Like a vase that runs a little waterfall
Onto the table—it has so many flowers.

She let him—made him—fill up every space.
Even when he gave her the article
On the women's triathalon, she had said,
"Oh, I don't have time for that,
And I'd rather spend the weekend with you."

She had traded herself for him
And now he was gone and she was empty
And had collapsed around her emptiness
Like a shopping bag without its bread.

It would not be a sin
For she would not be killing a living thing.
She would be weeding the garden
And the weed was dead and brown.
His love had been her greening
And her salvation.

She had searched herself
For something that was still alive
Even seeds she could soak

And she had found nothing.
Only pain would die.

Her children would be better off, surely.
Her brother who had them for a week now
Might keep them then.
She was a bare cupboard to their needs
A broken cup stained with bitterness.
They ought never to taste her again.

"Mama, can you French braid
my hair? Mama, what's the
matter? Braid my hair, can't you?"

"No, I can't, I can't, I CAN'T."

Oh, oh, oh, throw it away!

One desperate day with the want ads
Had made her future clear as a crystal ball:
She was not marketable.
Child support—if he paid—and a minimum
　　wage
From Safeway or the drugstore
Would form the piggy bank they would live
　　on.
She would do her best
To stay awake for an evening class
In maybe dental assisting
And come home to scream
At a child's smallest request.

She would be a little rubber band
Stretched thin to keep house
Job and children together

And if she had to add a broken washing
    machine,
Snapping!

Oh, throw it away, and do it now!

She turned on the water to fill the glass
And her eyes warily traveled up to the mirror.

Oh, God!

More than an exclamation, it was a prayer.

Please, don't let me look like that!

Her brown hair was oily and uncombed
And flat on the side she'd been lying on.
Her skin was red and puffy
And her eyes were shrunk and sunk in dark
    hollows.
The yellow bathrobe she'd had on for days
Was torn and tired and she'd hated it
Even when new, but could never justify
Getting a prettier one.

Oh, throw it away!

Her hand picked up the first red bottle
Then paused as she looked again at her face.
Jolene would be the one to find her.
To find her looking like *that?*

Jolene, president of the women's group
At church, had been calling daily
And needed or not was coming by that night.
A picture of what Jolene would find

Moved like a gust of cold wind through Sara's
    mind.
The least she could do was to tidy up a bit.

Sara filled the tub with hot water
Remembering as it was almost full
The bottle of bubble bath
Her twelve year-old daughter gave her last
    birthday.
She had been saving it for when
The little one needed a treat
But now she poured a little, then more
Then all and watched the bubbles foam
Their magic pink and gold as if she had
Never seen them before.

Sara lay soaking in the tub
Enjoying it as one enjoys the very last
Chocolate in the box.
She shampooed and conditioned her hair
Letting her fingers caress the scalp just
Like Tina's over at the beauty school
When she went in for a cut.

She hadn't taken a tub bath in maybe a year
Just quick showers because two minutes
Was all it sometimes took
For one child to maim another.

She got out and dried her skin slowly
And smoothed her body with lotion.
The hot rollers were ready and she put them in
Carefully including every hair.
She couldn't bear to put the yellow bathrobe
Around her soft, lotioned skin.

New wine in old bottles!

Wadding and stuffing it into the wastebasket
Made her laugh the first laugh she'd
Had in three months.
She would never need the yellow bathrobe
    again.

Throw it away!

Now, which dress? The blue one, of course.
People always told her she looked nice
In that dress. It matched her eyes.
Of course, her eyes would be closed
Or would they be open
And Jolene have to close them?

Slowly Sara took out the rollers
And brushed her hair
Teasing it a little to add some height
And trimming the bangs just a little there.

Eye shadow—lip liner—lipstick—mascara.
This would be her thank you to Jolene for
    caring.
She'd have to remember to lie down
On the couch so as not to muss her hair.
Perfume—lilac, her favorite.

There!

Sara reached again for the red pills
And poured them all into her hand
Then picked up the glass of water and—

Who was that woman in the mirror?
That woman with just a hint of a lover
On her lips and a hint of
A mountain climber in her eye.
Sara studied the woman
Then spoke in slow amazement:

    "You look too good to die!"

Suddenly a dam broke
And Sara was no longer empty.
She was filled with rage
Rage against whatever had made
That woman in the mirror feel like a weed
Rage against him for taking
Her power, rage against herself
For giving it away.

She threw the red pills against the wall
And they bounced into the bathtub.

    Throw it away!

They were not the soldiers!
She was the soldier
And she would win this war!

She grabbed the next bottle
And threw the pills against the wall.
Smash! The traitors!
She was not the enemy, but they nearly had
    her.

She would live!
She would fill herself
Quarter inches at a time
Until she was full and real and
Capable
    And beautiful
        And marketable!

The last of the pills hit the wall
And dropped into the tub
And she bent and turned on the water.
As she watched their little bodies
Swirl down the drain, the phone rang.

"Hello, Jolene? . . .
Yes, you can take me out to lunch. Surprise.
Right now. I'm already dressed.
Oh, anywhere. No . . ."

It must have sounded strange, she thought,
To hear a woman say with a voice
Shaking and sobbing,

    "I . . . want . . . Mexican!"

LAURA AND THE EMPTY TRAY

Sitting on the bench
Waiting for the bus
Laura looked like a person
Trying to look like the people
Who know where they're going.

Laura had been booted out of the house
By her husband
Whose last words to her had been
"I don't want to see you until five o'clock,
And don't you dare come home a minute
    sooner."
And then almost pleadingly
"Have a good time."

She had begged Stephen not to make her go
Not to make her spend a whole
Eight hours out there
Doing anything she wanted to do.
She was already doing what she
Wanted to do, and she didn't have
Time for anything else.

"But honey," he had said
"If there were more time
If another whole day were magically
Tossed into the week—
A day just for you—
What would you want to do?"

Laura's answer came as quickly
As the computer prints item and price
In the grocery store:
"The downstairs bathroom," she said.

There had been two cans of paint
Beside the tub for months.

White eyes staring accusingly
At the walls that were slowly peeling
And at Laura, who was running in and out
Trying not to think
About the paint and the tube of caulking
For the sink.

It was easy.
What would she do with another day?
The downstairs bathroom.

Stephen had taken her by the shoulders
And looked deep into her eyes
As if his own held a flashlight.
"Laura, where are you? Where are you?
I can't find the woman I love anymore.
She's lost. Help me find her."

Laura lowered her eyes and thought.
"Aren't we supposed to lose ourselves?
Isn't that what service is all about
Forget yourself and serve others?"

"No," he said. "It's not."
You're supposed to serve everyone
But you've been forgetting someone.
What can you serve from an empty tray?
How can you water plants from an empty
    pot?"

Laura started to cry.
When frustration began to well
Like the hot springs at her uncle's ranch

She always cried.
He was right. She had been going on empty
For a long time.
She had been reaching into herself
As into an apron to throw feed
To a yardful of chickens
And coming up with empty hands.
And the chickens cried louder
And sometimes she felt like wringing their
    necks
And sometimes like jumping over the fence
And running, running, running.

Stephen put his arms around her
And drew her close.
He hated to have her cry.
He would rather she yell or even hit.
But she always cried
And hid in some dark corner inside
That no flashlight could find
Making him stumble around in his search
Palms out for blind man's bluff.
So he took her in his arms
And Stephen cried too
Because he loved her.

"Look," he finally said
Pulling her down beside him on the couch.
"Next Wednesday will be your day.
Go out—do anything you want to.
I'll hire a babysitter and get off early—"

"Pay?" she interrupted
Looking at him like she looked at her children
When they suggested moving to Disneyland.

"A babysitter," he said quietly
"Is cheaper than a psychiatrist."
Laura began to cry again.
He was talking about Donna
A friend from where they used to live
Who they'd just learned had spent two
    months
In a psychiatric hospital.

How had it happened to her?
She had been the one who had done
Everything perfectly all the time
And done it with a smile—
Until she began kicking her children
And taking twice as much valium
As her doctor prescribed.

On Wednesday Laura was out of the house
By ten, telling the children
Something that was not quite a lie
And giving the babysitter the
Longest possible list of things to do.

And now, sitting on the bench
Waiting for the bus
Laura looked at her watch.
Where in the world could she go
For a whole day?
If she had the children with her
They could go to the zoo—she'd been
Promising to take them to the zoo for months.
She looked at her watch again.
What if she went back to the house
Climbed in the window downstairs
And did the bathroom?
No. Stephen would ask for a full report

And she couldn't lie.

Laura sighed, and the same feeling
Arose from the pit of her stomach
That comes with sitting in a traffic jam
When the dinner in the oven will be ruined
If it doesn't come out in fifteen minutes.

With everything she had to do—
Why—why did he make her—?

"I'll clean out my purse," she thought.
"I've been needing to clean out my purse."
Quick, efficient fingers emptied her bag
Putting the good things in one pile
And the junk in another—
Sugarless gum wrappers, old grocery lists
A petrified apple core
The arm of a Barbie doll
A program from last week's church service
And a handful of cracker crumbs.

She threw the rubbish
In a garbage can by the bench and shook
Out the empty purse.
There, that felt better.
At least she'd have something
To show for her day.
Why hadn't she brought the bills?
Stephen would never have noticed
If she'd stuffed the bills and envelopes
And stamps into her purse—she could have
Paid all the bills.

The bus arrived and Laura boarded.
Maybe downtown something would come to
    her.

Looking out the window, Laura filed her nails.
Good things she always carried
Her nail file around in her purse.
Then she did the eye exercises that
Once in a while she got around to doing.
Let's see. She didn't need a haircut.
Darn—if she'd brought her lists she could
    have
Gone to a phone booth and made her calls
For church and for the bake sale at school.

She looked at her watch again
And figured out what the babysitter had
    earned.
That feeling came again from her stomach
And she watched the babysitter's fee climb
Like you watch the meter at the gas station—
Fifteen cents—twenty cents—twenty-five
    cents.

The hot springs began to well again.
Why is he making me do this?
The bus passed the department store.
She could go in and get underwear
For Crissy, who had only two decent pair
But Stephen had made her promise
If she bought anything it would be for her.
The bus stopped and Laura got off
And looked around
Like someone in a strange airport.
Maybe she should have saved the arm
Of the Barbie doll. Oh, well.

Let's see. She could buy some pantyhose.
That would be for her.
But if she saved the money
She wouldn't feel quite so bad about
The meter at home soaring higher and higher.

Two blocks away was the library.
Darn—why didn't she bring the book
She had found under the couch—
Bedtime for Frances.
She had paid for it already
But maybe if she brought it back anyway
They would reimburse her—do they do that?
It wouldn't hurt to ask,
She had nothing else to do.

The walk to the library felt good.
It always felt good to walk with a purpose.
She opened the heavy door and was overcome,
As she always was, with the smell of the
    library—
That wonderful gluey smell that instantly
    catapulted
Her back into the excitement of adolescence
And school and learning
And looking at who else was there.
She'd always had to back in and out
Of library doors, for her arms were always
    loaded.
As Laura headed toward the desk
A display of paperbacks caught her eye.
To Kill a Mockingbird.
The title jumped out at her.
Just the other night she had driven
A group of high school girls home
From a volleyball game at the church

And they had been complaining about
Having to read *To Kill a Mockingbird*
Thirty pages a day.

Laura had laughed.
"Oh, boy—I wish your English teacher
Would assign me to read
To Kill a Mockingbird.
Wouldn't I love to have to read
Thirty pages a day?"

Slowly Laura reached out and picked up the
    book.
A smile crept over her face and she looked
    around
Like you do when you find money on the
    ground.
Could she? Would it be okay?
Stephen made her come.
It wouldn't be her fault.

Laura chose a chair with cushions
And opened the book as guiltily
As if it had just come in the mail
In a plain brown wrapper.

At twelve o'clock she had not
Shifted once in her chair.
At one o'clock she shifted in her chair
But forgot the peanut butter sandwich
And banana in her purse.
At two o'clock she did not know that
She was in a chair—or a library—
Or a mortal body.
At 5:08 she closed the book
And stared at the wall for minutes

Stared without seeing.
Suddenly she focused on the clock and
    jumped.
She was supposed to be home by five!

Quickly she put the book back on display
And then ran to the pay telephone by the
    door.

Her fingers easily found a coin
(Good thing she had cleaned her purse)
And she dialed her number.

"Hello?"
"Oh, Stephen, I'm so sorry.
I'll be home as soon as I can.
I came to the library to see
If they would reimburse me
For *Bedtime for Frances*.
But I forgot to ask them and I—
I read a book—I read a whole book, Stephen.
Stephen—are you there?"

"Laura?"
His voice was the voice you use
With your doctor after he has studied
All the tests.
"Laura? Did you have a good time?"
"Oh, yes. Oh, Stephen, it was wonderful!
I can't wait to tell you.
Oh, Stephen, thank you!"
Laura began to cry.
And Stephen cried too
Because he loved her.

Laura had to back out of the library door
For her arms were loaded.
Some of the books were for the children
But some were for her!

She ran the two blocks to the bus
Heavy—but not with books.
Full—like a tray, like a pot
Full like a farmer's apron
And she couldn't wait to throw it all
To the little chickens
And anybody else in the yard.

She had tomorrow all figured out.
Just think!—
A bathroom wall, then a book for the children
Then a chapter for her, then a bathroom wall
Then a book for the children
Then a chapter for her.
And then, if she really felt like it—the sink.

HISTORY'S AFFIRMATIVE ACTION

Of course it's not fair
But it may be karma.

Carma
Being a modern woman
Can butter her bread
On both sides
And have her cake
And eat it too
Or even butter her cake
On both sides
Which she is having
And eating too.

I mean
She can sue
Her employer for promoting
A less-qualified male
And on the way home
When she has a flat
Step out in her spikes and hail
The nearest man and bat
Her eyelashes so that
He gets grease on

And she never has to
Break a nail.

SINGLE

No one could believe Jenny
Was happy living alone
So she soberly accepted their sympathy
Like she accepted other
White elephants
She put in a big box
In the back closet
And thanked them very much

Then clicked the lock quick
As if hiding a secret

And ate a big salad
In front of the whales and dolphins
On PBS

And spent an hour
At her keyboard
Processing her words

And sat twenty minutes
At the window
Watching the storm dance branches

And stayed on the phone
An hour and a half
Until a hundred hungry Africans
Were fed

And then took a bath
Three chapters long

And slept smiling and sprawled
In her queen-size bed.

PICTURE WINDOW

Kathleen
Who was out of control
Like a slope of oranges
After someone has taken
Ten at the bottom
Looked enviously at

Susan
Who carried her stress
As gracefully as she carried
The perfect pie
She had brought to the meeting
Last Wednesday night.

Kathleen
Who yelled at her children
Even when they were not
In danger of oncoming cars
And who slammed the door
After she told her husband
To have it his way then
And who once a week at least
Locked herself in the bathroom
And cried
Called

Susan
Who never perspired
And who taught classes called
"Toward a More Feminine You"
And who smiled all the time
And whose children
Always got awards
To ask if she could

Come over sometime
To get a little help.

Kathleen
Who was so disorganized
That she went on Thursday
Instead of Friday
Got a lot of help from

Susan
Who happened to be
Out front in curlers
And wrinkled slacks
And wild-woman eyes
Screaming at her youngest child
Who had just batted a ball
Through the picture window
That framed the lamp
With the beautiful butterflies.

BREAKTHROUGH

She always ignored
The ring of her telephone
Like a private ignores
The bark of his sergeant.

So on the February day that she
Climbed out the upstairs window
To sit on the roof and be only feet
From the full-flowered Magnolia tree

And the telephone rang

And she did not jump and dive
But only stared
At the mass of purple-pink and white petals
Curled friendly around each other
Dancing gently on the air

And the telephone stopped

She sat there
AWOL and smiling.

NEXT TO GODLINESS

There are cobwebs behind my washing
    machine.
I never see them except when I lean
Over to take out the ironing board
Or to put it away.
And then there they are—
An incriminating network, thin and grey.

One day
In a fit of pride, I said to myself
"Look here, cleanliness is next to godliness
And a mere half-hour would make the
    backside
Of your washing machine so clean
You could eat off it."

I ran toward the closet
For the rags and soap and mop.
But I had to pass by the bookcase on the way
And right there on top—
Oh, you know the rest.

Well
There still are cobwebs behind my washing
    machine.
But when I lean
Over to take out the ironing board
Or to put it away
There is a thought that consoles:

Heaven's got to be more
Than a place scrubbed clean
For a bunch of cob-webbed souls.

THE HONOR

At two in the morning Launa May was nearly
    done.
If she used up the scraps she could get one
More that looked as good as the rest of them.
She twisted the wires of the artificial green
Around the carnation and pinched it into a
    stem.

The other women had helped until midnight
But Launa May had sent them home.
After all, she was head of the women's
    committee
For the church and it just didn't seem right
To make them all stay up
So she insisted on finishing the job alone.

She flexed her fingers and began:
"This fragrant flower comes to say . . ."
She finished the last line
Took a moment to rub the back of her neck
Where the muscles hurt
Then attached the card to the final flower
With the final pin.

"If you want a job done right
Just get the ladies to do it,"
Brother Nelson had said with a grin.
"Like I always say—where would we be
If it weren't for you?"

Launa May
Missed most of the program the following day
The songs of the children
And Brother Nelson's talk.

Her husband's elbow woke her just in time
To reach out and accept the corsage.
She pulled out the card:
"This fragrant flower comes to say
How we honor you on this Mother's Day!"

She looked up at the bright young man
Holding a basket in the aisle.
"Why, thank you. Thank you very much,"
She said with a smile.

TO ALL WOMEN EVERYWHERE

Let us sing a lullaby
To the heads of state.

They are our little boys grown up
And they have forgotten the sound
Of their mother's voice
And they need to be
Sat in the corner
Or given a good shaking.
Are they too big for that?

Then let us sing until their fingers
Fall from the fateful button
And they put the guns
And tanks back in the toy box
And remember that their mother
Told them we do not
Hurt one another.

Let us sing until they
Close their eyes
And dream a better dream.

Let us sing them to peace.

men and women

THE EMBRYO

Love is no eagle
Strong amid
The heights.
It is an egg
A fertile
Fragile
Possibility.
Hold it warm
Within your wing
Beneath your breast.

Perhaps in heaven
Love can live
Self-nourished
Free.
But in this world
Where mountains fall
And east winds blow
Oh, careful—
Love is embryo.

TOGETHER

Perhaps we can be together there
In that next place
Where bodies are so pure
They pass through planets—

Perhaps there
Where the light that lighteth the sun
Is kept on all night every night
And no one watches for morning
Holding the cold off with a candle—

There, perhaps
Where pain is exchanged
For peace and a memory—

You and I can touch as we pass
And gather in the good of one another.
We can love and give
In whatever loving, giving ways
There finally are.

We still will wish
To be together then, I think.
Perhaps then we shall know how.
Perhaps, even, we shall know why
We cannot be together now.

THE VALENTINE

I loved
The valentines we made in school.
I never cut the hearts out flat—
The two sides would never match for me.
I always folded and centered
And scissored out half a heart
That opened into perfect symmetry.
So they never had a side that was fat
And a side that was skinny.
I loved them for that.

I felt sort of nice and tidy that way
The day we saw the shape of our being one—
As if it had opened from some good design
That made two matching halves
Yours and mine.

But I find we don't stay put like paper.
We are not comfortable with glue.
Your edges have shifted, stretched
And mine have too—
But not to a pattern.
If we folded our halves up today
They would not fit.
Occasionally I itch for the scissors
I will admit.

Ah, well!
I will put away childish things—
Cut them off like braids.
We are no valentine, you and I.
We are something so alive, so moving
So growing, I can not yet
Put a name to the shape.

I only know it goes on and on and on
Pressing toward whatever border
There may somewhere be.

Your center and mine are one
And between the halves there is flow.
That is much.
I will let the edges go.

DOUBLE WEDDING

Let's have a double wedding,
You and me
And eros and agape.

Let us post
Interchangeable notes
On bedroom wall
And refrigerator:
"Love thy lover
And love thy neighbor."

Let us hold hands
In movies
And in the hospital.

Let us kiss
Shoulders and eyelids
And the cut fingers
Of small children.

Let us serve one another
Apple blossoms in vases
And quartered fruit
On trays.

Let us write poems
And wills to each other.

Let us have nights
As friendly lovers
And days as loving friends.

And let the four of us,
You and me

And eros and agape,
Stand in line together
At the grocery store
And at a golden
Anniversary.

LAST TOUCH

When she touched him for the first time
His skin was warm
And his hair was soft
And his fingers sweet
And the sun through the tall pines
Rose in invocation
On the blanket of blossoms
And he was so beautiful
And she had never seen such a smile.

When she touched him for the last time
His skin was cold
And his hair was thin
And his fingers shook
And the moon through the hospital window
Fell in benediction
On the little table
Heavy with flowers and fruit
And her tear joined his tear
At the little line
Where his smile began.

FLAWS

She was fed up
And ready to pack her bags
And might have hauled out the Samsonite
That very morning if she hadn't read
In the Sunday supplement how
Michaelangelo made the David
Out of a block of marble so flawed
That other sculptors passed it by.

So instead of leaving him a note
Telling him to go to hell
She sat in their room
In the reclining chair
Thinking up one nice thing to say
Which was that he always had clean hair
And then remembered too
That he was sweet to the kids
And that he laughed at her jokes
And that he didn't like his job
But every morning got up anyway.

And she remembered too
That she usually burned carrots
And didn't smell so great
In the mornings
And could stand to lose thirty pounds
And even her kids said
She'd forgotten how to play.

For two hours and a half
She sat there studying her marble
And measuring and figuring
And dreaming and sharpening her tools
For one more day.

AT THE ALTAR

The thought
Of forever
Teased my mind
Like a mountain
Through a thickly
Misted view.

But today the
Veil dissolved
To show—
Eternity
Is you.

EVE'S MEDITATION

Trunk and leaf
Make the tree,
Body and wing
Make the bee.

Gazing at the garden
I cannot think it odd
That you and I together
Make the image of God.

RELEGATED TO THE KITCHEN

In the front room
Grandfather and the men
Straightened ties and shoulders
Exchanged business cards
And solutions for the war
Slapped backs at jokes
And were very hungry.

And in the kitchen
Grandmother
And the aproned women
Warmed the hors d'oeuvres
And one another
Hugged, kissed cheeks
Touched each other's hair
Talked heartbreak and hope
And dreams of the day
And were filled
Before the filling
Of the first tray.

AFTER THE MASTECTOMY

They were afraid it would be different
To make love without
Her breast on
And it was.

Right from the start
It brought him closer
To her heart.

AND OBEY

He was the god of her world
He told her:
She was under him
As he was under God
Which left her
She soon realized
Pretty far under.

The person who drinks downstream
Of the cattle herd
Is less likely to get a clear drink
Than the person upstream.

But he
Being the god of her world
Blessed her with groceries today
And eternal exaltation tomorrow
And without him, they both knew
Whatever would she do?

Now
If I had been on the jury
For the crimes he committed
To which she closed her eyes
She would have been guilty too
Of course.

And
I don't defend her
Dumbly watching for ten years as
Her husband's cool hands
Took off his belt
With the silver buckle
To beat the kids.

Nor
Do I excuse her
Returning her parents' letters
Unopened or telling her friends
They could not call
Or speaking things that were not true
Because her husband told her to
Or eating only fruit
And wearing sleeves that reached her wrists
And never cutting her hair
Because her little god decreed
What she could do, eat, wear.

But
I say it is time
And way past time
That every woman
Invite herself upstream
Where the air is sharp
And the water is clean.

RADICAL

She could discuss issues
With the best of them
And did her part for the causes
Absolutely   .

But sometimes she left early
During refreshments
Or before the envelopes
Were all stamped
To go to another meeting

And her friends never guessed
She hurried home
Where
In a matter of hours

With one wonderful man
She established peace
Justice and equality
Ended hunger
And observed the triumph
Of love.

SUPPORTIVE WIFE

Her job was to be
A supportive wife

And so

Sometimes holding a noose
Around his neck

Sometimes working the strings
That played his ankles and elbows

Sometimes steadying the crutches
She placed under his arms

She stood
Supporting him as best she could.

FOR A DAUGHTER IN LOVE

I would not walk on her happiness
Any more than I would
Walk on a brand new lawn.
It is too tender.

I will not tell her now.

She has fallen in love
And I will wait until she has gotten up
And is standing straight.

I will wait until she comes to me
With questions in her eyes like tears.

I will tell her then
Like we finally tell the person
Who is sent out of the room
In those silly games we used to play
Tell her what everybody else
Has known, each in their turn:

That falling in love is a trap
Whereby life snatches people by the two's
And ties them so tightly together
That they can't get away
Until they learn something.
Learn about love, real love:
Being in, working in, living in
Rising in—all begun by
Falling in.

I hope she will be a good sport
And nod her head and even smile
And say, "Okay."

SECOND WEDDING

This time a woman
Not a girl

A necklace
Not a pearl

An orchard in September
Not a branch in May

Abundant with a hundred
Tumbling loves
Fruited and golden
To gift a man

She says "I do"
And knows "I can."

LETTING GO

I did it just like
The counselor said.
I closed my eyes
And saw myself on the pier
You on the boat
A rope between
Tied waist to waist.

"And now untie your end
Of the rope, slowly."

It felt like hemp in my hand
But I knew it was not.
Every fiber was an event
A laugh, a kiss, a fight
A prayer, a birth, a joke
A tear, all braided together
And tight.

"Let it go.
It's time to let go."

I looked at the boat
And could not read your face
In the shadow of the sail.

Through my hands
And into the water—
All that laughter
Those prayers
Tears, kisses in the water.

I would have jumped in
To save them
Like children overboard
But they were water
In the water now
And the boat was moving
And you were waving goodbye.

"Let go. It's through."

The boat bobbed
Further and further

And I waved too.

NOT A PAIR

Alison agreed
To become part of a couple
Not half of a pair.

A pair of skiis
Must ride the slope
Without a deviation
And if one makes
An independent motion
The jig is up.

A pair of socks
Must cling together
In the wash
And if one takes a spin
With the sheets or the towels
The other sits on the shelf
Flat and waiting for its match
To show up with the next batch.

Alison had been paired
Before and it scared
The daylights out of her to even think
Of linking up with anyone.

She had been a sock lost in the wash
Had been a ski that caused upsets on the
    slope,
And she wasn't now about
To become a glove.

But she loved him
And he loved her
And they decided "couple"

Was a word roomy enough
That they could both live in it.
It had two syllables, anyway
Instead of one
And it even sounded like dancing
Which, these days
Lets you be
Both together and free

All
Over the hall.

THE RAIN AND THE GROUND

He was the rain
And I loved him for this.
He brought the flowers
I knew they were his.

He moved over me
A gentle storm
The rain was sweet
And the rain was warm

And the flowers came
And the flowers grew.
That he brought the flowers
Was all that I knew.

Drought has come
And drought has burned
But nature teaches
And I have learned:

I am the ground
No matter the skies.
Oh, I bring the flowers
And the flowers will rise.

POSITION

If "A" looks up to "B"
Then by nature of the physical universe
"B" must look down on "A"
Rather like two birds
Positioned
One on a tree
And one on the ground.

Or so thought Marjorie
Who had always wanted to marry
A man she could look up to
But wondered where that
Would place *her*
If she did.

Imagine her astonishment
When she met Michael and found
That together they stood
Physics on its head.

You could never
Draw this on paper
For it defies design

But year after year
They lived a strange
Arrangement
That by all known laws
Could not occur:

She looked up to him
And he looked up to her.

motherhood,
pregnancy, and birth

NEEDED

The earth needs
Only nature.
If spring follows
Snow
If new seeds
Swell
Earth will go
On and on
Content.

I have watched
With folded hands
An uneasy guest.

But now
Suddenly
I am nature.
And I am needed
As all tomorrow's
Orchards
Need the present
Tree.

How good—
This nine-month
Indispensability.

CHILD MAKING

She knew that if she had to
Hand-make this child

She would probably end up
With something like
The dress with the huge arm holes
She hid half finished
In the bottom drawer

Or the plaque on the kitchen wall
From which beans and corn
Kept dropping:

A child
With far too much skin
Or eyebrows
That just would not stay on.

So she lay back
And day after day
Knitted away
On little booties
   (uneven but sweet)

Glad she had help
In making the feet.

DAY-OLD CHILD

My day-old child lay in my arms.
With my lips against his ear
I whispered strongly, "How I wish—
I wish that you could hear.

"I've a hundred wonderful things to say
(A tiny cough and a nod)
Hurry, hurry, hurry and grow
So I can tell you about God."

My day-old baby's mouth was still
And my words only tickled his ear.
But a kind of a light passed through his eyes
And I saw this thought appear:

"How I wish I had a voice and words;
I've a hundred things to say.
Before I forget I'd tell you of God—
I left Him yesterday."

DON'S DAUGHTER

I celebrate the birth
Of this girl child
With the joy
Of a Hebrew celebrating
The birth of a boy.

With tambourines
Or cards or calls
Her birth
Is worth
Celebrating:

See how her mother smiles
(Though that is no surprise)
But, oh
See how her father
Kneels at the cradle
Of this little goddess
With worship in his eyes!

THE NINTH MONTH

Being a duplex
I have been happy, my dear
To loan you half the house
Rent-free and furnished
As best I could.

You have been a good
Tenant, all in all
Quiet, yet comfortably there
Tapping friendly on the wall.

But I hear
You have outgrown the place
And are packing up to move.
Well, I will miss
The sweet proximity.
But we will keep in touch.
There are bonds, my dear
That reach beyond a block
Or a mile or a hemisphere
Born of much love and labor.

I approve the move
And gladly turn from landlady
To neighbor.

NEW CHILD

I savor
This mutual feast:

You
At my breast
Desperately
Drinking life

And me
Watching
Touching
Sipping eagerly
On your sweet
Evidence
Of immortality.

adoption

TO AN ADOPTED

I
Did not plant you,
True.
But when
The season is done—
When the alternate
Prayers for sun
And for rain
Are counted—
When the pain
Of weeding
And the pride
Of watching
Are through—

Then
I will hold you
High,
A shining sheaf
Above the thousand
Seeds grown wild.

Not my planting,
But by heaven
My harvest—
My own child.

ON PURPOSE

The little girl unfrowned and then
Sort of smiled when
After hearing the dictionary definition

She was told that what adopted
Really meant was

Searched for
Prayed for
Worked for
Finally gratefully got
Unquestionably on purpose
And loved a lot.

parenthood and
child raising

DIAPERING AT 4:00 A.M.

I saw a calf born once.
It really was amazing
How soon (all tidied up by tongue)
He wobbled off
And the new mother
Went back to grazing.

But you, my little creature
At the top of the animal kingdom
You would lie in the pasture for months
And wave your fists and cry.

So here we are
You and I
Tied together in all
The bathings and the dryings
The pickings up and the puttings down
And the turnings over
The dressings and the undressings
And the powderings and the feedings
And the cleanings up of the comings out.

I know—
I know what it's all about
This disguised blessing of unavoidable touch
Spinning a thousand threads
That encircle us like little lariats.
And before you know it
We're caught.

Calves come for going.
But not—not my little ones.
The Lord thought it all up
This essential intimacy

And He called it good.

He created the heavens and the earth
And the seas, and the naked, needing
Infants crying to be held.
He thought it all up
This clever stratagem.

And yet—
I'll bet He smiled
When He thought about diapering at 4:00
A.M.

BANKERS

He works at the bank
And has a large desk
And people listen when he talks.

And he takes good care .
Of his charges:
Money, certificates
Stocks.

And she stays home
Unnoticed
And every day
Tends treasures
That outshine all the gold
In Fort Knox.

MOTHER TO CHILD

Look—
Your little fist
Fits mine
Like the pit
In a plum.

One day
And one size
These two hands will
Clasp companionably.

Help me, child.
Forgive me
When I fail you.
I'm your mother
True
But in the end
Merely an older equal
Doing her faltering best
For a dear
Small friend.

PROTECTION

Take my hand
Child—
There are dangers
At our feet.

I grope
The uneven ground
Through mist
Fearfully and slow.
But you—
(Oh, take my hand)
You go
With unsuspicious eyes
With trusting walk.

There are dangers
At our feet
And I see them all.

Take my hand
Child—
Lest I fall.

THE VOW

How could I hide you
From hate?
I would
Though my arms break
With the trying.

Life leans in
At the window there
With its bag
Of dark treasures
Trying for your eyes
So utterly open
So unaware.

You will see
Men smile over blood
And you will know
There is hate.
You may see bombs
And butcheries
And you will know
There is horror.

Against all this
What can I do?
Only vow
That before you
Leave my arms
You will know
Past ever doubting
That there is
Love, too.

TO A CHILD GONE

I thought I was ahead of you in line.
You would take your turn
After I took mine
Like we did before.

I guess you don't need new shoes
For starting heaven
Or a light left on against the dark
The way I always did.
But I'm so used to parenting.
I wanted just to be there
To do whatever needed to be done.

But you went first.
And now, my little one
Suddenly you are my senior.
Morning, I know, will come.
But bring close your light—
This time it is I who fear the night.

MOTHERLOAD

Motherhood has ruined me for life.

I want to nurse the world
A continent to a breast.

I want to cut up waffles
For all the third world
Send the dictator to his room
Ground the drug dealers
Wash out the pornographers'
Mouths with soap
And spray organized crime
With Black Flag.

I want to make all the politicians
And all the executives sit on the couch
And memorize the golden rule
And stand up and say it in unison.

I want to grab a bullhorn
And announce to the world
That the barbecues will stop
Until all the litter—*all* the litter—
Has been picked up.

Oh, I could fix everything
If they would all just listen to me,
Listen to me,
Listen to me!

I have such illusions of grandeur:
I am a mother.

AARON'S OTHER WOMAN

Clearly it takes
Two generations of women
To civilize a man.

I took him past
Throwing food on the floor
Peeing in public places
Saying bad words
Spitting on the sidewalk
And playing on the escalators.

But I could never
In a million mother years
Take him the quantum leap
This seventeen year-old girl
With the wispy telephone voice
And the lavendar eyelids
Has taken him in one week:

Taken him by a slim
And bracleted arm
Past belching, grunting
Scowling, snapping

And into smiling, sweetness
Singing
And infinite charm.

TO MY TEENAGER

What do I do with a child
Who is taller than I?

How quickly you passed
My navel, my shoulder
My chin, my nose.
And now there is
No more of me
To measure you by.
You are off the chart
And it has thrown things
All askew.

How do you look up to tell a person
What to do?

You can look down and say
"Hey, the radio goes off now."

Height
Means "Now hear this!"
At least pulpits
And stands and stages
Assist in underlining
Amplifying
And being taken seriously.

I have lost my pulpit.
How can I preside?
Future shock is in my eyes
As I look up and ask if you
Would be willing to
Turn down the radio
Please?

DON'T PUSH

The minute the doctor said "push"
I did, and I've got to stop now
Because you're eighteen.

Breathe deeply
Think of something else
Don't push
Don't push.

MOTHER'S POST PLEDGE

Look,
I hereby:

Cross out my critique
    of your performance,
Toss out my agenda
    for your life,
Tear up my list of
    things you need to do,
Swear up and down
    I will not do it again.

Of course it's odd,
But for a while there
I mistook myself for God.

JOHN LEAVES HOME

Surely you're not going without me?
Surely you're not taking your stereo
And leaving your mother?
Surely, John, a policeman will find you
And bring you home.
We're not finished!

I read to you *The Little Red Hen*
And talked about industry.
I read to you *Animal Farm*
And talked about equality.
But I have not read to you yet
Les Miserables
Or the complete works of Shakespeare,
And if I don't
Who will?

I have discussed with you at the dinner table
My hundreds of news clippings
On American-Russian relations
Acts of heroism and horror
The birth of a panda
And Ann Landers' columns on
Drug abuse, sending thank you notes
And teenage pregnancy.
But next month and the next
Newspapers will come out
And if I don't scour them for things
You need to know about
Who will?

I have made you turn off the TV
Left a list of important things to be done
In your blue color-coded notebook

On the kitchen counter:
"Mow lawn, sweep back deck, vacuum
    bedroom,
Write letter to grandparents, get haircut."
But the days will continue to come
With their twenty-four hours
And if I do not write out for you
A list of important things to do
Who will?

Ah, you are laughing.

Oh, John, take me with you.
Tuck a little mother in your head
And every now and then let her speak.

Take me with you.
You need to cease being a child
But I need always to be a mother
And if you won't let me
Who will?

OBEDIENT GIRL

Everybody was proud of this little girl.
She loved to please and obey.
She got good grades
And she baked good cakes
And she cleaned her room each day

(And she came home pregnant at seventeen).

She loved to please and obey.

FOREVER CHILD

She holds her big girl
Across her lap on the couch:
Rocking chairs were not made
For children who will be
Forever children.

She spins words of comfort
Like a song—
Maybe tomorrow, maybe tomorrow,
Maybe tomorrow it will be possible

To stand up in the roller skates

To speak words that others understand

To find a friend who would like to
Go to a movie this weekend

Maybe tomorrow, maybe tomorrow.
Lullabies were not written
For children who will be
Forever children.

And she looks out the window
At the darkening sky
And closes her eyes and prays again
That she will outlive her sweet baby:

The world was not made
For children who will be
Forever children.

PATH OF A PARENT

It starts with
Meditation on the toes of a baby
And leads to spiritual exercise
That would break the best yogi
Sitting cross-legged before his lotus:

Serenity
And colic
And three hours sleep last night

Grace
And the puppy feces
On the new carpet

Charity
And screams
In the grocery store when the
Oreos are ripped from white knuckles

Harmony
And three Halloween costumes
By tomorrow morning:
A clown, a witch
And a washing machine
To go with Stacey's dryer.

Honor
And another conference
With the teacher
And possibly the principal

Silence
And the roar of motorbike
And rock

And tap shoes on kitchen tile

Acceptance
And all that is dear
Packing up and leaving home

Path to god-consciousness
All begun by
Meditation on the toes of a baby.

FOR CHILDREN GROWN AND GONE

My garden could not contain
The beauty of you.

I watched you blossom
Then burst into blessings,
Seeds winging in the wind
Beyond my field.

Only God can measure the yield
Or knows
All the places where
Your beauty grows.

THE MOTHER THE HARBOR

These little boats
Came by currents
I may never know
From oceans I cannot see
Even from my highest hill.

I cherish the cargo
Bless the sea
And thank the eternal itinerary
That harbored them awhile
In me.

adversity

TRIAL NUMBER FIVE

Carefully they laid
Out on the table
Trials one, two, three,
Four, five, and six.

"Choose one," they said.

"Oh, any," she cried, with a horror
Born of the best of Halloweens,
"Any but number five.
It would kill me.
I promise you I would not survive."

They thanked her graciously,
Escorted her out,
Then gift-wrapped, addressed,
And labeled "Special delivery"
Trial number five—

Sent with love from
Those whose assignment it is
To make sure you know
That you can go
Through trials one, two,
Three, four, ninety-nine,
Or five—
And, incredibly,
Come out alive.

SHORT ROOTS

The tree
At the church next door to me
Turned up its roots and died.
They had tried
To brace its leaning
But it lowered
And lowered
And then there it lay—
Leaves in grass
And matted roots in air
Like a loafer on a summer day.

"Look there"
Said the gardener
"Short roots—all the growth went up—
Big branches—short roots."

"How come?" I asked.

"Too much water.
This tree had it too good.
It never had to hunt for drink."

Especially in thirsty times
My memory steps outside
And looks at the tree
At the church next door to me
That turned up its roots and died.

TIME FOR THE GULLS

It's time, Father
For the gulls, I think.

My arms shake
From flailing my field.
I sink
Broken as the little stalks
Beneath their devouring burden.

I yield it all to you
Who alone can touch all things.
It's time, Father
For the gulls.

I will be still
And listen for their wings.

GOOD GROUND

I have seen love
Fallen on unbroken ground
Blow with the first wind.

I have seen love
Laid in a shallow row
Unearthed with the lightest rain.

But pain
Is a plow
That opens earth for planting.

My heart is ready now.
Hurt-furrowed, it has depths
Designed for sowing.

Oh, love that lands here
Finds good ground for growing.

THE PEARL

The little grain of sand
Is planted
And an ancient urge
Begins its work.

I, the unhappy oyster
Settle in the sea and curl
Defensive luster after luster
Around the pain—
Reluctantly
Pregnant with pearl.

MIRACLE

To the unseen angel
Who holds to my breathing soul
The blessed anesthesia
Much thanks.

I sense the surgery
But do not feel it.
Stay close
Until time can heal it.

A DRAMA IN TWO ACTS

I dim
I dim
I have no doubt
If someone blew
I would go out.

I did not.
I must be brighter
Than I thought.

LABOR

You have come in
Like a wounded animal
That crawls into a log
To die.

Now
Do not think me
Unfeeling.
It's just that I have
Been through it
So many times
And seen it
So many times
And know
I'll see it again.

I will hold your hand.
But if you see me
Smiling just a little
While you're writhing and torn,
Please understand
That I know labor pains
When I see them—

And frankly, I can't wait
To see what is struggling
To be born.

STILL LIFE

The first thing she did
When she walked in the door
After the doctor talked about
Six months if she was lucky

Before she read the leaflet
Clutched in her hand on chemotherapy

Before she called her sister

Before she sat on the couch and stared

She went to the back closet
And unwrapped the easel
And the oils that were still good
Which the children had given her
Several Christmases ago.

And set them up in the kitchen
Where the afternoon light hit
Her little garden in a pot
Her little African violet.
She studied the seven purple flowers
With five golden knots
As though embroidered at each center.
She studied the thirteen green velvet leaves
And the underside where the vulnerable
Red veins ran.
She had never seen anything more beautiful

And she began.

service

HE WHO WOULD BE CHIEF AMONG YOU

And he rose from supper
Poured water in a basin
And washed the disciples' feet.

Those hands
Hardened by the heat of a desert sun
Comfortable with cutting trees
And turning them to tables
In Joseph's shop—

Those hands
That with a wave could stop
The troubled sea
Could touch a leper clean,
Or triumphantly turn death away
From the loved daughter on Jairus' couch—

Those hands
That could gesture the heavens open—
Poured water in a basin
And washed the disciples' feet.

The lesson lies unlearned
But to a few
Who trust the paradox
And hear the call:

"He who would be chief among you,
Let him be the servant of all."

GIVING

I love giving blood.
Sometimes I walk in
Off the street
When no one has even asked
And roll up my sleeve.

I love lying on the table
Watching my blood flow
Through the scarlet tube
To fill the little bag
That bears no address.

I love the mystery
Of its destination.
It runs as easily
To child or woman or man
Black or white
Californian or Asian
Methodist, Mormon
Muslim or Jew.

Rain does too.
Rivers do.
I think God does.
We do not.

Our suspicious egos clot
On the journey from "Us" to "Them."

So I give blood
To practice flowing
Never knowing
Where it's going.
And glad.

SERVICE

Who casts bread upon
The waters in crumbs
Recieves it back
In loaves.

And who casts
The bread in loaves
Receives it back
In banquets.

healing and comfort

THE HEALING

A bird
Once broken
Can never fly
They say
Quite so high
Again.

Perhaps.

But as for me
Now desperately
In need of mending
 I have a healer
Who would restore
These foolish wings
Without a scar.

I will lie quiet
Beneath His touch.
I will listen
As He whispers
"Rise
And fall no more."

And then—
Then I shall
Soar.

BLESSING

Spirit hands are on my head—
Father, Mother blessing me.
Comfort courses down like rain
Cleansing and caressing me.

CHRIST CHILDREN

Let us make you a child again
For Christmas.
Let us put you in the cradle
As we put Jesus in the manger
Pre-crucifixion and sweet
With just-born eyes that meet
The wonder of star and smile.

For a little while
Let us make you children again.
Here there are no nails
In your innocence.
Here there is over you
A sky bursting bright
And under you the breast of a mother
Softer than hay.

You will not stay
I know
And Jesus will have to go
To Golgotha:
His little hands were born
To bear a cross.
And you, my darling,
Came to the same sad world
Where trust is lost
At the hands of those who
Know not what they do.

At the end of the story
The Christ will rise
And so will you.

But let us make you
Children again for Christmas
(The Christ children that you are)
Touched only by swaddling
And the light of a star.

PURIFICATION

If the sea
And the sun
Can bleach a bone
Till it's whiter
Than a gull
Cleaner than foam—

Oh, how bright
My soul
Can emerge
Purged
On the beach
Of Christ's water
And light.

And—

How calm
And warm
His sand.

old age

TO AN AGED PARENT

"Here, Dad—
Let's tuck in the napkin
Just in case."

    The spoon makes its
    Hazardous trip to your mouth
    And you glance at my face
    To see if I notice.

"All clean?
Grab hold then—up you come."

    I dry your body from the bath
    And tell of things I saw downtown
    To turn your mind from modesty.

"Now, if you need something
Just ring the bell.
I'll leave the door a little open
And turn on the hall light.
Good night."

    You close your eyes
    And curl into privacy
    Free from the indignities of the day.
    "Sister, don't ever grow old"
    You used to say.
    And here you are.

    Oh, Daddy, Daddy—
    There's no way to stop it
    Or to slow it.
    Let's just let it be.

Time's strange circle
Has brought around your turn
To be comforted and cleaned
And nursed.
Shhhhhh—it's all right.
Let me hold you warm
In your last days
As you did me in my first.

WOMAN AGING

All her life she had been
A vegetable garden
Every inch rowed and planted
In corn, beans, carrots:
Producing
Nourishing
Doing.

Now some landscape architect
Has rearranged the space
Clearing, softening
Putting in a little pond
And a path and sand
Offering a quiet place
For being
For sitting on the one rock
And studying
The single lotus.

Pastel and thin
She is an Oriental meditation garden
Designed for going within.

death and beyond

OF PLACES FAR

To me Istanbul
Was only a name
Until a picture
You took
Of the Blue Mosque
Came.

I don't receive
Postcards from heaven
Showing Saint Peter
At prayer
But, oh—that place
Is real enough
Now that
You are there.

POINT OF VIEW

Sun and mountain meet.
"Look," I say.
"Sunset!"

But I forget
That far away
An islander
Wipes morning
From his eyes
And watches
The same sun
Rise.

What's birth?
And death?
What's near
Or far?
It all depends
On where you are.

GOD SPEAKS

Death is ugly?
Oh, my children.
No.

If you knew
That beauty
That begins where
Your sight fails
You would run
Run, run
And leap
With open arms
Into eternity.

But sad
Is a harvest
Of green wheat.

And
So you would
Feverishly
Cling to earth
And finish
Your mortal task
I merely gave
Death
An ugly mask.

VITAL SIGNS

How presumptuous we mortals are
Pronouncing one another dead
Because the eyes are closed
The lips are stilled
There is no motion in the narrow bed.

A man once came
To clear our definitions.
He knew all words, all places
All states of being
For he had traveled below all things
And above.

"Death," he said, "is darkness, is hate."
"And life," he said, "is light, is love."

Oh, look again.
A vital sign burns bright and gives
This word:

She loved, she loves, she yet will love.
And Love pronounces that she lives.

indexes

Index of Titles

Index of First Phrases